SEEDS IN OUR SOULS | CHRIST AT OUR CORE

A collection of poems by Kally Reynolds

SEEDS IN OUR SOULS | CHRIST AT OUR CORE

ISBN 979-8-3302-5080-6
Ebook ISBN 979-8-3302-5081-3

Cover photograph by Joanne West
< jwestphotography.com >

Interior design and layout by Jackie Casey
< jecruby.com >

To contact the author:
< kallyreynoldscafe@gmail.com >

Author's Note:

I wrote these poems in response to the great anxiety and divisiveness I see and feel all around me, especially here in the United States. These reflections came to me in a four month period in which they practically flowed onto the page. They are, in a sense, my reflections to and with you, my fellow travelers, as we sojourn on this crazy, yet glorious home we call Earth. They are also, in a sense, love letters, not only to you, but to Jesus Christ, who died, and still lives, to set us free.

I live with my husband, Jim, in Gold Canyon, AZ, and with our tomcat, Tommy TC. I've worn many hats in my life including (but not limited to): teacher, crisis communications consultant, certified coach and P.R. director for a major bedding company. I have also edited numerous books and written many columns and magazine articles, along with one book about dating after divorce*. This is my first book of poetry.

*Of Frogs & Princes: Reflections on Relating,
Dating and Mating for Women Who Have Been There Before

A sower went out to sow his seed; and as he sowed, some fell along the path and was trodden under foot, and the birds of the air devoured it...And some fell among thorns; and the thorns grew with it and choked it. And some fell unto good soil and grew, and yielded a hundred-fold.

--- Luke 8:5, 7-8

God is our refuge and our strength, an ever-present help in distress. Therefore, we fear not, though the earth be shaken and the mountains plunge into the sea...

--- Psalm 46:1-2

For my beloved family and friends, and for Jim Reynolds,
my daily inspiration and the love of my life.

Table of Contents

Telling the Tale

We talk of unfaithful lovers
and friends who prove false,
all while Your Spirit hovers
and gives us a choice.

Shall we breathe in the Spirit
of Your all-abiding Love;
do we touch, taste and hear it –
this Love from above?

Is it Good News or Bad News?
Our lives tell the tale.
Are we freed by God's Spirit
or boxed up in jail?

Do we groan in confusion,
regrets far and near?
Are we caught in illusions
or freed from our fear?

For You love us regardless
our choice for the day:
heart-filled or heartless,
we go on our way.

Everything but That

Have I died, Lord?
I didn't know it.
If that's the case,
I think I've blown it.

I've lived for me
and not for You –
and lived this way
my whole life through.

While "dying to self"
sounds mighty fine,
I think I'll keep,
my own life mine.

Set your minds on things above, not on earthly
things. For you have died, and your life
is hidden with Christ in God.
--- Colossians 3:2-3

I get, O Lord...

I get, O Lord, that You
are God.
Although I think it
very odd
with You so big and
me so small,
that You would care for
me at all...
That it would matter
what I do
to a God so big as You.

Come Again

Lord, I'll do whatever
you say....Call my name,
and I will follow.
So why, in the world, does
my love feel hollow?

Lord, I'll do whatever
You ask. Just make it loud
and crystal clear –
or, better yet, Lord,
will you just reappear?

Rescue

O Lord, please rescue me
from my craving for diversions.
For what can be important
when everything is urgent?

Be it on-line games or
Facebook, texts, TV or the phone,
all crowd out the sacred space
meant for us alone.

O Lord, help me seek You,
at dusk and light of day,
to dethrone the diversions
that sabotage my way.

Vision

You fret you don't do much
to bring God's kingdom
down to earth...
You fret you're a slacker,
and your life's of little worth.

You celebrate the New Year
but fret it all the same.
For hollow are resolutions
when you are steeped in shame.

But shame's a jealous jailer.
It will not let you see
how dearly you are known and loved,
nor that you've been set free.

Once you really see your worth,
you'll bring God's kingdom down to earth.
So dwell not on your tiny frame,
but on the God who knows your name.

Question

Where does love go
when it grows cold?
Does it turn into ice
or morph into mold?

What does love do
when it turns away?
Does it jet to the shore
or stay home and pray?

Wise or foolish –
how can I say?
But is love really love
when it goes away?

The Gift

I'd like to write
a simple poem
with words that soar
yet cut to the bone.

A sonnet fair,
a glimpse of gold,
a moment that
would ne'er grow old.

But modest verse
instead I write –
and this is not
an oversight.

It is my gift,
however small;
I give it, Lord,
I give it all.

I give this verse
to You today
with all I do
and all I say.

Give me, Lord, the
eyes to see and
the heart to love
who's next to me.

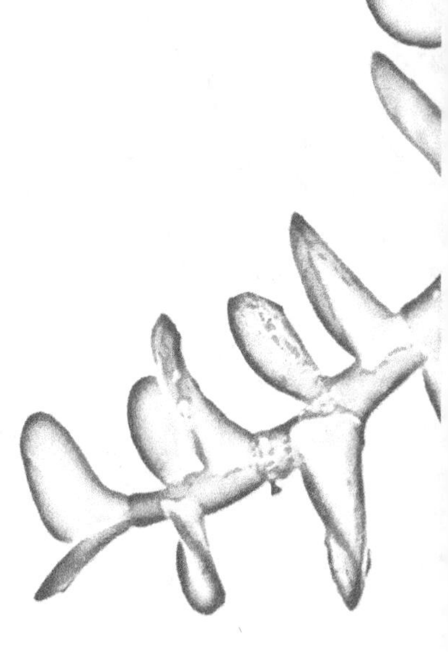

Allegiance

Craven fear bows down to sin –
be it lust or greed or pride.
The sin itself, it matters not.
Fear would have us hide.

At first it asks for little,
this craven fear we serve;
but then it spreads its poison,
and we do not have the nerve.

The trade-off starts so easy,
it's hard for us to tell that
we're not "safe" by heaven's gate,
but on the road to hell.

Proof of Life

I cannot prove I love you
although I am your wife;
yet let my heart be wise enough
to show you with my life.

But even then you may doubt
or love me not so true.
I cannot prove in a courtroom
that I'm in love with you.

Christ couldn't prove he loved us,
although he really tried
with signs and miracles he did
up to the day he died.

But even if he so loved then –
and some claim he lives today –
it takes more than courtroom proof
to melt our doubts away.

A Word from Jesus

You fear you love me not enough
to walk with Me today;
to transform the cares and challenges
that will doubtless come your way.

And yes, I know these doubts of yours,
your cave-ins and your wiles.
But don't forget, my darling,
you are my precious child.

So come to Me when you are weak,
and ask me to replace
your cave-ins and distractions
with My ever-present Grace.

The Battlefield

On many morns, my soul feels fraught;
there seems no way to free it.
I hear the news – I get the blues,
and pray for a better way to see it.

For many moons, it's gotten worse –
vile hatred and brazen lies –
that even though I try to love,
I'm almost paralyzed.

Where in the world does Truth flee
when bludgeoned by these lies?
Hated, hounded and hunted,
where does Truth go to hide?

But once I ask the question,
Love comes to me and says,
"Look not below, nor in the clouds,
but look to Me instead.

"I am the Lord of Love and Truth,
which always intertwine.
Trust in Me and let me help you
win the battles in your mind."

On the anniversary of my mother's death

This Day

We live in a time of fierce conflict,
but also a time of fierce grace.
We live in a time of fierce trauma,
more than we think we can face.

Yet, this day we can make a difference –
this day is of infinite worth.
This day we can do the little things
that matter right here on earth.

This day we can sing our love songs –
our love songs to our King –
sharing God's Kingdom here on earth,
and that means everything.

Ode to a Long-Gone Professor

Professor Meade, I did believe
your words, they hurt me so.
You said my verse was bad or worse
than grimed-up city snow.
And so it went, 'til decades spent,
I asked, "What did you know?"

Dear Doctor Meade, I do believe
your words – they've helped me so:
a lesson learned, a gift I've earned,
for now I truly know.

My songs are fit, a candle lit,
no more are they in hiding.
A blind man's eyes once hypnotized
and stopped me from my writing.

But Thomas Meade, it wasn't you
that made me still my voice.
It took me years, and many tears,
to admit I had a choice.

Even Then

What's a sin
and what is not?
Ten Commandments,
it's what we've got.
To this number
more were added
(and, I'll guess,
some were padded).

God gave us Ten,
but then the Law grew,
so Jesus boiled
it down to two:
love our God
over every other --
father, sister,
mother, brother.

Love each other
even when....
Yes, love each other,
even then.
Help the stranger,
even when.....
Yes, help the stranger,
even then.

Impossible

Have you ever done something
you think was "Impossible" –
that is, without landing
right in the hospital?

I've climbed giant redwoods,
kept my balance on highwires.
And when my husband left me,
ran a marathon through the mire.

I liked to imagine
I had done the impossible,
until meeting the Messiah
in the four Hebrew Gospels.

With no home or money,
no royal friends or fame,
Jesus died two thousand years ago;
yet, billions know his name.

Some use it as a curse word
some say it as a prayer;
yet, even now, in modern times,
His name is everywhere.

Don't you find that peculiar,
strange and mighty odd?
Could it be He really IS the
Living Son of God?

Perspective

How do I make peace
with someone I despise?
Even though I see him not,
he tramples through my mind.

I even curse his name sometimes,
when his name is being said.
I know this isn't Christian,
but I wish the man were dead.

Jesus says to hate the sin,
but then to love the sinner.
I'm on board with number one,
but the second is no winner.

Lord, tell me how to love a man
who's evil through and through?
Who'll never change his evil ways –
who'll never come to You?

Lord, please give me the insight
and the rare courage to see
my sins in the cold light of day,
and the grace You give to me.

Fantasies of Faith

We cannot live without faith,
no matter how we try.
We must believe in some things
and think others are a lie.

Sometimes we are so very sure
what we believe is true!
It makes us blind – and unkind –
and we do not look to You.

Sometimes we go to Scriptures
to find answers we think best;
we read what we want to read
and proceed to skip the rest.

Yes, many go to the Bible --
(yes, many claim this is safest),
reading just the parts that give them heart,
then shut God's Book, still racists.

Contagion

Are we called to fight evil
wherever we find it?
I think that we are,
but, Lord, please remind me.

How can we prevail over
all the hatred we see,
without hating the haters
or wanting to flee?

It's so easy to hate haters,
for their hatred's outrageous –
but hard to remember,
it's also contagious.

Feeling It

Feelings are curious creatures
of every shape and size.
Still, all have this in common:
they want to rule our lives.

Feelings insist they must be true
for they've known us from the start:
if only we put our trust in them,
they'll protect our minds and hearts.

Yes, feelings are persuasive,
with that certain kind of glow.
Yet no matter how much I trust
in them, doesn't make it so.

Some feelings I must take to heart
and others, soundly ditch.
This is all quite clear to me –
but not always, which is which.

Conversations with Jesus

"Wounded people all around you,
wounded people who you see;
sense the brokenness around you,
bring their brokenness to Me.

"Yes, the wounded all surround Me,
wounded people everywhere,
trying hard to hide their sorrows,
carrying burdens they can't bear.

"Wounded people all around you,
wounded people who you see –
love the people who surround you,
bring their brokenness to Me."

"Lord, it's hard to love the wounded,
when I am so wounded too.
Where can I find the heart to love them,
if I don't bring my wounds to You?"

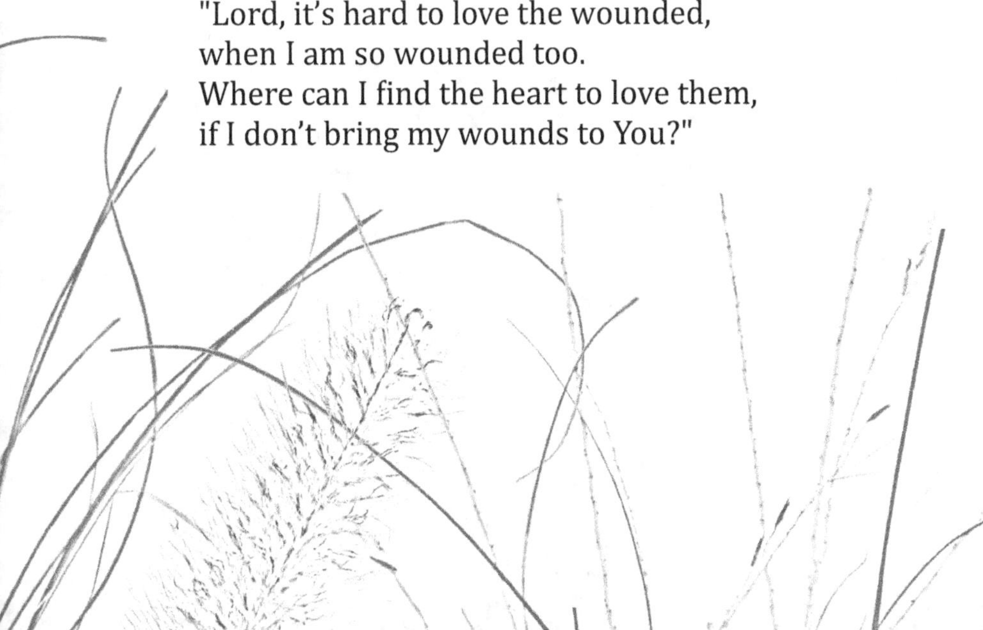

Grace

Grace is what we don't deserve --
I've always thought that true --
but, maybe, just maybe,
God wants me to love me too.

"Love your neighbor as yourself,"
Jesus says we're bound.
I can't love you when I hate me.
Is grace where love is found?

If grace, then, is our birthright,
this treasure from above,
everything in this crazy world
can help us learn to love.

More Than a Feeling

Fear is the feeling,
appearing as a friend,
warning us of dangers
that just could spell THE END.

But, alas, like friends
who prove to be false,
we followed their counsel,
we trusted their voice –
only to learn that fear
steered us wrong,
robbed us of courage
and cut short our songs.

The fear of what others
say is often a clue;
their fear is contagious
and not really true –
nor are the whispers:
"Don't plant the seeds;
don't take the actions;
don't do the deeds.

"It's safer, by far, to
stay small, safe and tame.
You'll fail, in any case,
for you're weak and you're lame."

Still, fears can be true friends
that enable us to thrive.
We ignore them at our peril –
for they keep us alive.

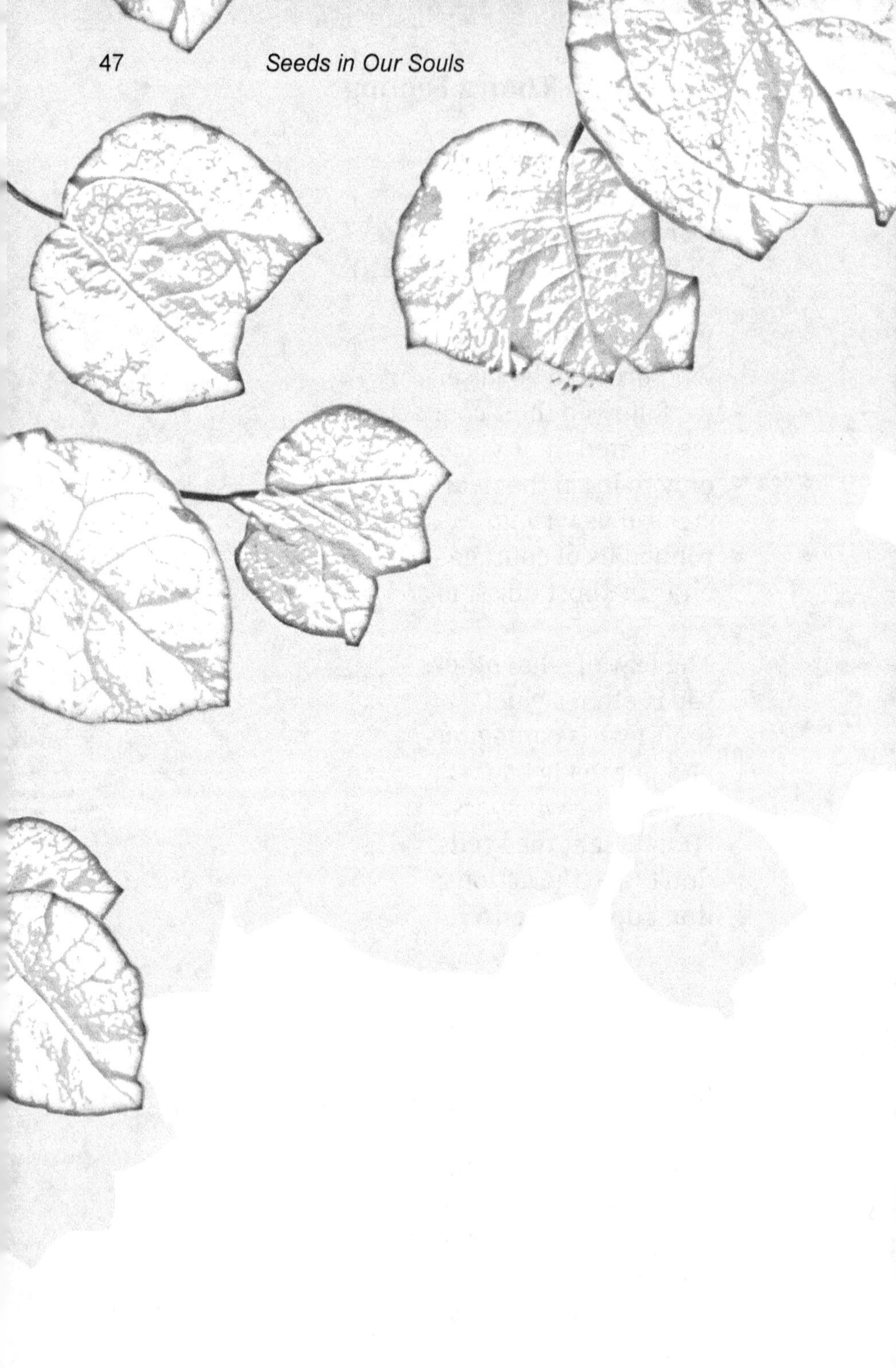

An Inconvenient Truth

Family or friend?
Foe or stranger?
For some I feel love,
with others, danger.
For most I feel little
or nothing at all –
just nameless humans
passing by in a mall.

Family or friend?
Foe or stranger?
Which are you, Lord –
You, born in a manger?
Do I see you in others?
Yes, maybe a few...
Yet, mostly, I don't.
Please, give me a clue.

Family or friend?
Stranger or foe?
I'm only human
so how could I know
the countless people
who You love so?
For some are so greedy,
some are so prideful --
these sinners disgust me,
these sinners You died for.

My small circle keeps
life easy and free –
unless I remember
You died to save me.

Mind Games

So many things
I thought were true
really weren't.
What about you?

So many warnings
now I find.
Still I refused
to change my mind.

What was the moment,
the moment you saw,
that what you believed
wasn't true at all?

Did you ignore it –
try to erase it?
or stop in your tracks
and squarely face it?

So many warnings
and yet we stay blind.
What does it take
to change your mind?

What If...

A case could be made
I'd be much the same
if our paths never crossed
and I knew not your name.

We'd have gone through our lives,
mere strangers we'd be,
if I'd never met you
and you hadn't met me.

Yes, a case could be made,
but it wouldn't be true--
for my life changed forever
the day I met you.

An Inside Job

Fear has a fierce energy
that can seem both meek and kind –
a well-bred way of acting
when you've really lost your mind.

"The cost's too great," fear whispers,
"and what if you are wrong?
You can't make any difference –
the evil is too strong."

I always used to wonder how
concentration camps could flourish --
until I vowed I'd speak out,
but didn't have the courage.

Last Day

What if last night
you came back from the dead,
learning that heaven
was just like Christ said?

But you couldn't stay
long here – only a day:
who would you tell?
What would you say?

Now, sure that Love is
of infinite worth,
what would you do on
your last day on earth?

Bottom-line

It takes awhile
to realize what
we are born to do...

Or else sometimes
we face our death
and find we never knew.

But either way,
no matter what,
Love will make the call.

The Love we share
in God's eyes will
matter more than all.

Seeds

Joy of my being,
Heart of my soul,
how can I share
You who I know,

in such a way
others will see
the depth of Your Love
for them and for me?

I want to do "big" things,
yet my seeds are so small!
Some days my best efforts
seem like nothing at all.

But feelings aside,
when it's Your Love I sow,
no matter how tiny,
these seeds will grow.